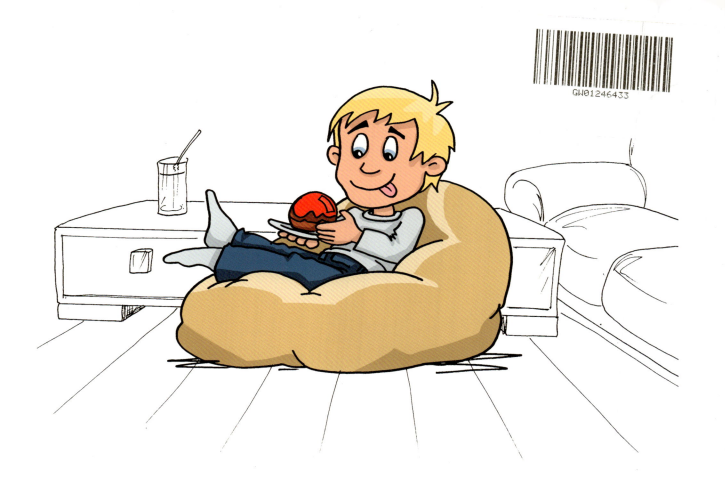

Tom has a red jam bun.

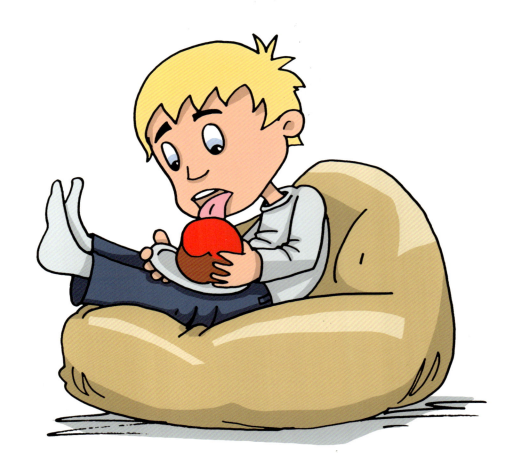

Tom licks the jam.
Yum, yum.

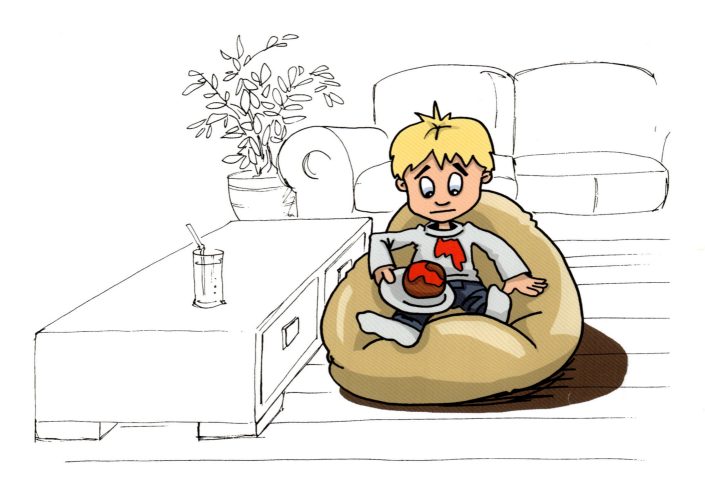

The jam drips on
Tom's top

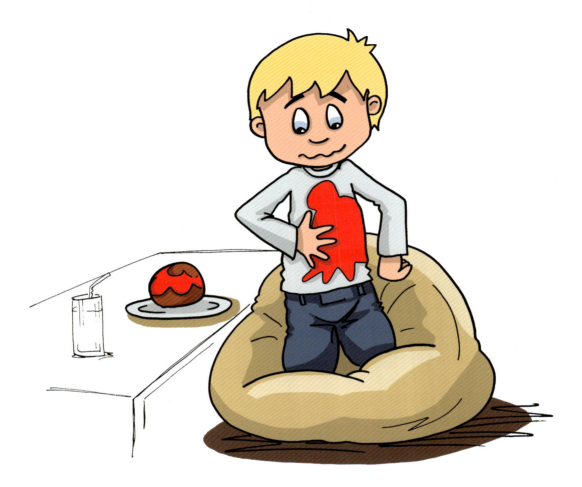

Tom rubs the jam.

His top is a mess.

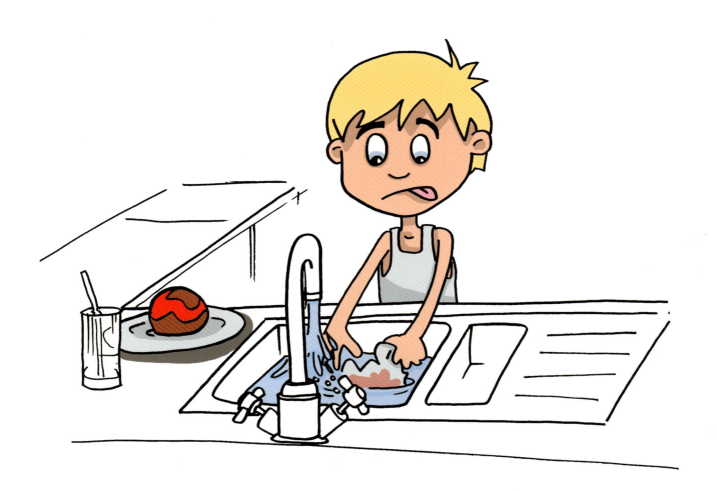

Tom puts his top
in the sink.

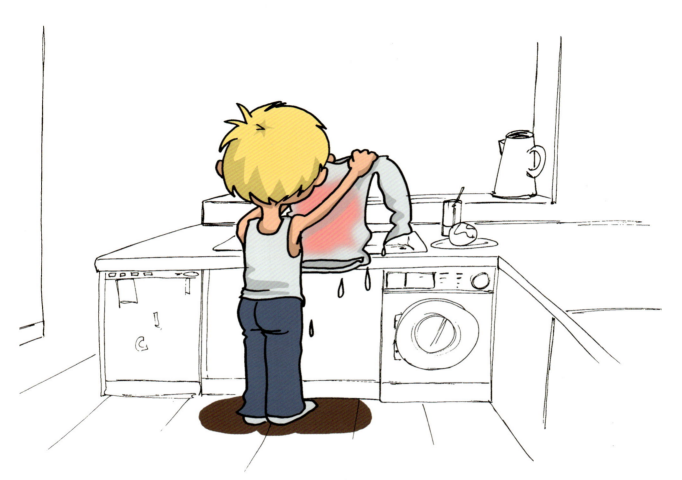

Tom rubs it. Oh no!

The top is pink.

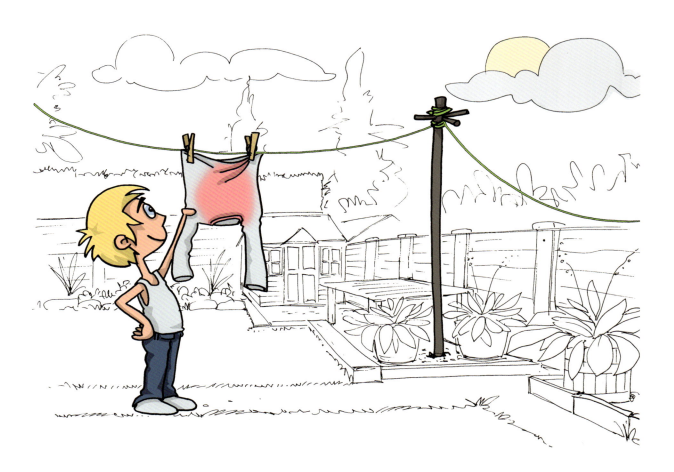

Tom puts the top in the sun.

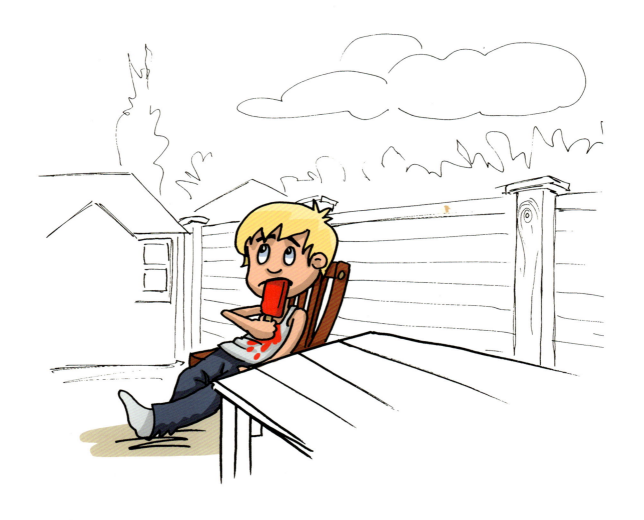

Tom has a red lollipop.